The Wicke

of

CRAZY
JOKES

The Wicked Book
of
CRAZY
JOKES

p

This is a Parragon Book
This edition published in 2002

Parragon
Queen Street House
4 Queen Street
Bath BA1 1HE, UK

Produced by Magpie Books, an imprint of
Constable & Robinson Ltd. London

Copyright © Parragon 2001

ISBN 0-75259-383-8

A copy of the British Library Cataloguing-in-Publication Data
is available from the British Library

Printed and bound in Italy

Contents

Introduction

What kind of person thinks his bath is electric because it has a plug? An idiot, that's who. And as you will learn from these pages there are an awful lot of them about doing some pretty crazy things. But just beware: word tricks can make you or a friend look a bit of a fool too . . .

Creatures Great
and Small

A woodpecker was pecking a hole in a tree. All of a sudden a flash of lightning struck the tree to the ground. The woodpecker looked bemused for a moment and then said: "Gee, I guess I don't know my own strength."

What do you get it you cross a hedgehog with a giraffe?
A long-necked toothbrush.

There was once a puppy called May who loved to pick quarrels with animals who were bigger than she was. One day she argued with a lion. The next day was the first of June.
Why? Because that was the end of May!

What kind of cats love water?
Octopusses.

Why does a stork stand on one leg?
Because it would fall over if it lifted the
other one.

First flea: You don't look too well.
Second flea: I'm not really feeling up to
scratch.

My dog saw a sign that said: "Wet Paint" –
so he did!

What's a porcupine's favorite food?
Prickled onions.

My dog is a nuisance. He chases everyone
on a bicycle. What can I do?
Take his bike away.

What's an American cat's favorite car?
A Catillac.

What's black and white and makes a lot of
noise?
A zebra with a set of drums.

What is a snail?
A slug with a crash helmet.

What should you do if you find a gorilla
sitting at your school desk?
Sit somewhere else.

What did the stupid ghost call his pet
tiger?
Spot.

Teacher: Who can tell me what geese eat?
Paul: Er, gooseberries, Sir?

Mary had a bionic cow,
It lived on safety pins.
And every time she milked that cow
The milk came out in tins.

Why should a school not be near a chicken farm?
To avoid the pupils overhearing fowl language.

Teacher: Martin, put some more water in the fish tank.
Martin: But, Sir, they haven't drunk the water I gave them yesterday.

What were the only creatures not to go into the Ark in pairs?
Maggots. They went in an apple.

What do you get if you pour hot water down a rabbit hole?
Hot cross bunnies!

What do you get if you cross a galaxy with a toad?
Star Warts.

On which side does a chicken have the most feathers?
On the outside.

Which bird is always out of breath?
A puffin.

What's the best thing to give a seasick elephant?
Plenty of room.

What sort of fish performs surgical operations?
A sturgeon.

Just before the Ark set sail, Noah saw his two sons fishing over the side. "Go easy on the bait, lads," he said. "Remember I've only got two worms."

What's a twip?
What a wabbit calls a twain ride!

Baby skunk: But, Mom, why can't I have a chemistry set for my birthday?
Mother: Because it would stink the house out, that's why.

Waiter, waiter, there's a dead beetle in my gravy.
Yes, sir. Beetles are terrible swimmers.

Keith: Our teacher's an old bat.
Kevin: You mean he's bad-tempered?
Keith: Not only that, he hangs around us all the time.

A teacher took her class for a walk in the country, and Susie found a grass snake. "Come quickly, Miss," she called, "here's a tail without a body!"

The Stock Market is a place where sheep and cattle are sold.

How do you catch a squirrel?
Climb up a tree and act like a nut.

Which animals do you have to beware of when you take exams?
Cheetahs.

Why did the elephant paint her head
yellow?
To see if blondes really do have more fun.

How many skunks does it take to make a
big stink?
A phew!

What was the fly doing in the alphabet
soup?
Learning to spell.

What happened when the headmistress's
poodle swallowed a roll of film?
Nothing serious developed.

What did the neurotic pig say to the farmer?
You take me for grunted.

What did the beaver say to the tree?
It sure is good to gnaw you.

Why don't centipedes play football?
Because by the time they've got their boots on it's time to go home.

What's the difference between a coyote and a flea?
One howls on the prairie, and the other prowls on the hairy.

Donald: My canary died of flu.
Dora: I didn't know canaries got flu.
Donald: Mine flew into a car.

How do fleas travel from place to place?
By itch-hiking.

What do you get if you cross a yeti with a kangaroo?
A fur coat with big pockets.

What do you get if you cross a cow and a camel?
Lumpy milkshakes!

What do you get if you cross a sheep-dog and a bunch of daisies?
Collie-flowers!

What do you get if you cross a zebra and a donkey?
A zeedonk.

What do you get if you cross a sheep and a rainstorm?
A wet blanket.

What do you get if you cross a vampire with a flea?
Lots of very worried dogs.

There were two mosquitoes watching blood donors giving their blood. "It's not fair," said one to the other. "They're happy to lie down and let someone drain a pint of blood, but if we zoomed down for a quick nip, they'd do their best to kill us."

An elephant ran away from a circus and ended up in a little old lady's back garden. The lady had never seen an elephant before, so she rang the police.
"Please come quickly," she said to the policeman who answered the phone.
"There's a strange looking animal in my garden picking up cabbages with its tail."
"What's it doing with them?" asked the policeman.
"If I told you," said the old lady, "you'd never believe me!"

What do you get if you cross a centipede and a parrot?
A walkie-talkie.

Two caterpillars were crawling along a twig when a butterfly flew by. "You know," said one caterpillar to the other, "when I grow up, you'll never get me in one of those things."

What dog smells of onions?
A hot dog.

What lies on the ground 100 feet up in the air and smells?
A dead centipede.

What did the grape do when the elephant
sat on it?
It let out a little wine.

What do you call a flea that lives in an
idiot's ear?
A space invader.

What do ants take when they are ill?
Antibiotics.

Who conquered half the world, laying eggs
along the way?
Attila the Hen.

Why was the young kangaroo thrown out by his mother?
For smoking in bed.

When is it bad luck to be followed by a black cat?
When you're a mouse.

The psychiatrist was surprised to see a tortoise come into his office. "What can I do for you, Mr Tortoise?" asked the psychiatrist.

"I'm terribly shy, doctor," said the tortoise, "I want you to cure me of that."

"No problem. I'll soon have you out of your shell."

Two fish were swimming in a stream when it began to rain. "Quick," said one fish to the other, "let's swim under that bridge, otherwise we'll get wet!"

What do you get if you cross an owl with a vampire?

A bird that's ugly but doesn't give a hoot.

"Who's been eating my porridge?"
squeaked Baby Bear.
"Who's been eating my porridge?" cried
Mother Bear.
"Burp!" said Father Bear.

Why are skunks always arguing?
'Cos they like to raise a stink.

If twenty dogs run after one dog, what
time is it?
Twenty after one.

Rabbits can multipy – but only a snake can
be an adder.

How did Noah see to the animals in the Ark?
By flood-lighting.

What swings through trees and is very dangerous?
A chimpanzee with a machine-gun.

What has four legs, whiskers, a tail, and flies?
A dead cat.

Have you ever seen a man-eating tiger?
No, but in the café next door I once saw a man eating chicken!

First cat: How did you get on in the milk-drinking contest?
Second cat: Oh, I won by six laps!

A man who bought a dog took it back, complaining that it made a mess all over the house. "I thought you said it was house-trained," he moaned.
"So it is," said the previous owner. "It won't go anywhere else."

Sign in shop window:
FOR SALE Pedigree bulldog. House-trained. Eats anything. Very fond of children.

Why couldn't the butterfly go to the
dance?
Because it was a moth-ball.

What do you get if you cross a flea with a
rabbit?
Bugs Bunny.

What do you get if you cross a crocodile
with a flower?
I don't know, but I'm not going to smell it.

What do you call a multi-storey
pig-pen?
A styscraper.

How can you tell if an elephant has been sleeping in your bed?
The sheets are wrinkled and the bed smells of peanuts.

Did you hear about the boy who sat under a cow?
He got a pat on the head.

Why do elephants have flat feet?
From jumping out of tall trees.

Is the squirt from an elephant's trunk very powerful?
Of course – a jumbo jet can keep 500 people in the air for hours at a time.

How do you make an elephant sandwich?
First of all you get a very large loaf . . .

What has two tails, two trunks and five legs?
An elephant with spare parts.

Mean and Nasty Jokes

The garbage men were just about to leave the street when a woman came running out of the house carrying some cardboard boxes.

"Am I too late for the garbage?" she called.

"No, lady," replied one of the men. "Jump right in!"

A woman woke her husband in the middle of the night. "There's a burglar downstairs eating the cake that I made this morning."

"Who shall I call," her husband said, "Police or ambulance?"

Girl: Did you like that cake Mrs Jones?
Mrs Jones: Yes, very much.
Girl: That's funny. My mom said you didn't have any taste.

Fred: I was sorry to hear that your mother-in-law had died. What was the complaint?
Ted: We haven't had any yet.

When you leave school, you should become a bone specialist. You've certainly got the head for it.

My Auntie Maud had so many candles on her last birthday cake that all her party guests got sunburnt.

When Wally Witherspoon proposed to his girlfriend she said:
"I love the simple things in life, Wally, but I don't want one of them for a husband."

Two friends were discussing the latest scandalous revelations about a Hollywood actress.
"They say she likes her latest husband so much she's decided to keep him for another month," said one to the other.

Roger was in a very full bus when a fat woman opposite said, "If you were a gentleman, young man, you'd stand up and let someone else sit down."

"And if you were a lady," replied Roger, "you'd stand up and let four people sit down."

My son's just received a scholarship to medical school – but they don't want him while he's alive.

My mother uses lemon juice for her complexion. Maybe that is why she always looks so sour.

My Auntie Mabel has got so many double chins it looks like she is peering over a pile of crumpets.

Chuck: Do you have holes in your underpants?
Teacher: No, of course not.
Chuck: Then how do you get your feet through?

My girlfriend talks so much that when she goes on holiday, she has to spread suntan lotion on her tongue.

At my piano teacher's last performance the audience cheered and cheered. The piano was locked!

A school inspector was talking to a pupil. "How many teachers work in this school?" he asked.
"Only about half of them, I reckon," replied the pupil.

Father: Would you like me to help you with your homework?
Son: No thanks, I'd rather get it wrong by myself.

I wouldn't say our English teacher is fat, but when she got on a Speak Your Weight machine it surrendered.

Rob: I must rush home and cut the lawn.
Teacher: Did your father promise you something if you cut it?
Rob: No, he promised me something if I didn't!

She's such a gossip she tells you what you were going to say to her before you have the chance to tell her.

I have two noses, three eyes and only one ear. What am I?
Very ugly.

Mrs Broadbeam: Now, remember, children, travel is very good for you. It broadens the mind.
Sarah, muttering: If you're anything to go by, that's not all it broadens!

Why is a caretaker nothing like Robinson Crusoe?
Because Robinson Crusoe got all his work done by Friday.

"Did you see him?" asked the policeman.
"No," said Mrs Blenkinsop, "but I'd know
that laugh anywhere."

What do you get if you pour boiling water
down a rabbit hole?
Hot cross bunnies.

I can't get over that new beard of yours. It makes your face look just like a busted sofa.

Henry: I'd like to learn to play a drum, Sir.
Music teacher: Beat it!

Yes, I do like your dress – but isn't it a little early for Hallowe'en?

You must think I'm a perfect idiot.
No, you're not perfect.

Soprano at concert: And what would you like me to sing next?

Member of audience: Do you know "Old Man River"?

Soprano: Er, yes.

Member of audience: Well go jump in it.

I don't care who you are, get those reindeer off my roof.

I don't know what it is that makes you stupid but whatever it is, it works.

My dad is rather tired this morning. Last night he dreamed he was working.

Wife: Shall I give that tramp one of my cakes?
Husband: Why, what harm has he ever done us?

My uncle spent a fortune on deodorants before he found out that people didn't like him anyway.

What is small, pink, wrinkly, and belongs to Grandpa?
Grandma.

Why do gorillas have big nostrils?
Because they have big fingers.

Why don't you go home and brush up on
your ignorance?

How does your head feel today?
As good as new.
It should be as good as new – it's never
been used.

My uncle must be the meanest man in the
world. He recently found a crutch – then
he broke his leg so he could use it.

I've got a good idea.
Must be beginner's luck.

I reckon Mom must be at least 30 years old – I counted the rings under her eyes.

Woman: If you were my husband, I'd poison your coffee.
Man: And if you were my wife, I'd drink it.

Visitor: You're very quiet, Jennifer.
Jennifer: Well, my mom gave me 10 cents not to say anything about your red nose.

Mom! There's a man at the door collecting for the Old Folks' Home. Shall I give him Grandma?

I've just finished painting your portrait. There, don't you think it looks like you? Er . . . well . . . it probably looks better from a distance.

"I told you it was like you!"

The new office-boy came into his boss's office and said, "I think you're wanted on the phone, sir."

"What d'you mean, you think?" demanded the boss.

"Well, sir, the phone rang, I answered it and a voice said, 'Is that you, you old fool?'"

Billy: I never had a sled when I was a kid.
We were too poor.
Milly, feeling sorry for him: What a shame!
What did you do when it snowed?
Billy: Slid down the hills on my cousin.

Do you think, Professor, that my wife
should take up the piano as a career?
No, I think she should put down the lid as a
favor.

Why did you refuse to marry Richard,
Tessa?
'Cos he said he would die if I didn't and I'm
just curious.

My Peter keeps telling everyone he's going to marry the most beautiful girl in the world.
What a shame! And after all the time you've been engaged!

Doctor Sawbones speaking.
Oh, doctor, my wife's just dislocated her jaw. Can you come over in, say, three or four weeks time?

"How should I have played that last shot?" the bad golfer asked his partner.
"Under an assumed name."

May I go swimming, Mommy?
No, you may not. There are sharks here.
But Daddy's swimming.
He's insured.

Alfie had been listening to his sister practice her singing. "Sis," he said, "I wish you'd sing Christmas carols."
"That's nice of you Alfie," she said, "why?"
"Then I'd only have to hear you once a year!"

Nurse: Doctor, there's an invisible man in the waiting-room.
Doctor: Tell him I can't see him.

A naughty child was irritating all the passengers on the flight from London to New York. Finally, one man could stand it no longer. "Hey kid," he shouted, "why don't you go outside and play?"

A scoutmaster asked one of his troop what good deed he had done for the day. "Well Skip," said the scout. "Mom had only one dose of castor oil left, so I let my baby brother have it."

Accountant: I'm having trouble sleeping – any suggestions?
Doctor: Have you tried counting sheep?

The apprentice electrician was on his first job. "Take hold of those two wires, Alex," said his master, "and rub them together." Alex did as he was bid, and his master said, "Do you feel anything?"

"No," said Alex.

"That's good – so don't touch those other two wires or you'll get a nasty shock!"

A rather stern aunt had been staying with Sharon's parents, and one day she said to the little girl, "Well, Sharon, I'm going tomorrow. Are you sorry?"

"Oh yes, Auntie," replied Sharon. "I thought you were going today."

Mr Brown: I hate to tell you, but your wife just fell in the wishing well.
Mr Smith: It works!

Did you hear about the woman who was so ugly she could make yogurt by staring at a pint of milk for an hour?

"Some girls think I'm handsome," said the young Romeo, "and some girls think I'm ugly. What do you think, Sheila?"
"A bit of both. Pretty ugly."

You're ugly!
And you're drunk!
Yes, but in the morning I'll be sober!

I don't think these photographs you've
taken do me justice.
You don't want justice – you want mercy!

Food and Physical Jokes

Jane's father decided to take all the family out to a restaurant for a meal. As he'd spent quite a lot of money for the meal he said to the waiter, "Could I have a bag to take the leftovers home for the dog?"

"Gosh!" exclaimed Jane, "are we getting a dog?"

A fat girl went into a café and ordered two slices of apple pie with four scoops of ice cream covered with lashings of raspberry sauce and piles of chopped nuts. "Would you like a cherry on the top?" asked the waitress.

"No, thanks," said the girl, "I'm on a diet."

Why is it that when I stand on my head the blood rushes to my head but when I stand on my feet the blood doesn't rush to my feet?

You're feet aren't empty.

Mom: Eat up your roast beef, it's full of iron.

Dottie: No wonder it's so tough.

A woman telephoned her local newspaper to let them know that she had just given birth to eighteen children. The reporter didn't quite hear the message and said, "Would you repeat that?"

"Not if I can help it," replied the woman.

Neil: I've changed my mind.
Jim: About time, too. Does the new one work any better?

You should get a job in the meteorology office.
Why?
Because you're an expert on wind.

That boy is so dirty, the only time he washes his ears is when he eats watermelon.

Waiter! Is there soup on the menu?
No, sir, I wiped it off.

Waiter, how long have you worked here?

Six months, Sir.

Well, it can't have been you who took my order.

What happened to Lady Godiva's horse when he realized that she wasn't wearing any clothes?

It made him shy.

Doctor, doctor, I think I'm a spoon.

Sit over there, please, and don't stir.

Doctor, doctor, my son's just swallowed some gunpowder!

Well, don't point him at me.

Doctor, doctor, I'm at death's door!
Don't worry, Mrs Jenkins. An operation will soon pull you through.

Doctor, doctor, Cuthbert keeps biting his nails!
That's not serious in a child.
But Cuthbert bites his toenails.

Nicky and Vicky were talking about a famous, very glamorous film star. "What do you think of her clothes?" asked Nicky.
"I'd say they were chosen to bring out the bust in her," replied Vicky.

Why did the farmer plow his field with a steamroller?
Because he planned to grow mashed potatoes.

Doctor, I keep stealing things. What can I do?
Try to resist the temptation, but if you can't, get me a new television.

Doctor: Good morning, Mrs Feather. Haven't seen you for a long time.
Mrs Feather: I know, doctor. It's because I've been ill.

How did the baker get an electric shock?
He stood on a bun and a current ran up his leg.

Do men always snore?
Only when they are asleep.

Doctor, doctor, how can I stop my cold going to my chest?
Tie a knot in your neck.

Doctor, doctor I keep losing my memory.
When did you first notice that?
When did I first notice what?

Some people say the school cook's cooking is out of this world.
Most pupils wish it was out of their stomachs.

Waiter, waiter, why is my apple pie all mashed up?
You did ask me to step on it, sir.

Did you hear about Lenny the Loafer? He is so lazy that he sticks his nose out of the window so that the wind will blow it for him.

What did the dinner lady say when the teacher told her off for putting her finger in his soup?
It's all right, it isn't hot.

Brian: How did you manage to get a black eye?
Bertie: You see that tree in the playground?
Brian: Yes.
Bertie: Well, I didn't.

Waiter, waiter, have you got frogs' legs?
No Sir, I always walk like this.

Ben, sniffing: Smells like UFO for dinner
tonight, chaps.
Ken: What's UFO?
Ben: Unidentified Frying Objects.

Statistics say that one in three people is
mentally ill. So check your friends and if
two of them seem okay, you're the one.

Doctor, doctor, my wife thinks she's a
duck.
You better bring her in to see me straight
away.
I can't do that – she's already flown south
for the winter.

What kind of beans do cannibals like best?
Human beans.

Did you hear about the two fat men who
ran in the New York Marathon?
One ran in short bursts, the other in burst
shorts!

Doctor, doctor, I think I'm invisible.
Who said that?

Did you hear about the dentist who
became a brain surgeon?
His drill slipped.

What do traffic wardens like for tea?
Traffic jam sandwiches.

Cannibal boy: I've brought a friend home
for dinner.
Cannibal mom: Put him in the fridge and
we'll have him tomorrow.

What is a dimple?
A pimple going the wrong way.

What happened to the man who put his
false teeth in backwards?
He ate himself!

What is the most popular food served at a
nudist camp?
Skinless sausages.

What's the best thing to put into a pizza?
Your teeth.

Ronald had broken a rib playing rugby. He went to the doctor, who asked how he was feeling. "I keep getting a stitch in my side," he replied.

"That's good," said the doctor. "It shows the bone is knitting."

Why did the old lady cover her mouth with her hands when she sneezed?
To catch her false teeth.

There was a fight in the fish-and-chip shop last night – a whole lot of fish got battered!

Doctor, doctor, I keep seeing double.
Take a seat, please.
Which one?

What kind of jokes does a chiropodist like?
Corny jokes.

Doctor, doctor, I think I've been bitten by a vampire.

Drink this glass of water.

Will it make me better?

No, but I'll be able to see if your neck leaks.

Which vegetable goes best with jacket potatoes?

Button mushrooms.

How can you tell an old person from a young person?

An old person can sing and brush their teeth at the same time.

Why are fried onions like a photocopying machine?
They keep repeating themselves.

My auntie has a sore throat. What should she do?
Take aunti-septic.

Who's stronger than a muscleman who can tear up a telephone directory?
Someone who can tear up a street.

Ben's new girlfriend uses such greasy lipstick that he has to sprinkle his face with sand to get a better grip.

Waiter: And how did you find your meat, sir?
Customer: Oh, I just lifted a potato and there it was.

Doctor, doctor! I'm becoming invisible!
Yes, I can see you're not all there.

What happens if you tell a psychiatrist you are schizophrenic?
He charges you double.

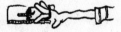

Waiter! What is that fly doing on my sorbet?
Learning to ski, sir.

A man who tests people's eyes is called an optimist.

The kidneys are infernal organs.

Why did the orange stop rolling down the hill?
It ran out of juice.

Doctor, doctor, I've only got fifty seconds to live.
Just sit over there a minute.

Did you hear about the girl who got
engaged to a chap and then found out he
had a wooden leg?
She broke it off, of course . . .

Doctor, doctor, it's wonderful! I feel like
my old self again.
In that case we'd better start a new
course of treatment.

My uncle's got a wooden leg.
That's nothing. My auntie has a wooden
chest.

How do you make gold soup?
Use fourteen carats.

Waiter, waiter, there's a bird in my soup.
That's all right, sir. It's bird-nest soup.

Waiter, waiter, this coffee tastes like mud.
I'm not surprised, sir, it was ground only a few minutes ago.

"I'm sorry," said the surgeon. "But I left a sponge in you when I operated last week."
"Oh," said the patient, "I was wondering why I was so thirsty all the time."

"Ugh! You smell terrible," said a doctor to a patient.

"That's odd," said the patient, "that's what the other doctor said."

"If you were told that by another doctor, why have you come to me?"

"Because I wanted a second opinion."

Trevor came rushing in to his dad.

"Dad," he puffed, "is it true that an apple a day keeps the doctor away?"

"That's what they say," said his dad.

"Well, give us an apple quick – I've just broken the doctor's window!"

"The sign says 'breakfast at any time,' so I want French toast during the Renaissance."

Jimmy was caught by his mother in the pantry. "And what do you think you're up to?" she asked furiously.

"I'm up to my seventh jelly tart," said Jimmy.

Now then, Deirdre, eat up all your greens like a good girl. They're good for your complexion, you know.

But I don't want to have a green complexion.

A man sat on a train chewing gum and staring vacantly into space, when suddenly an old woman sitting opposite said, "It's no good you talking to me, young man, I'm stone deaf!"

"The trouble is," said the entertainer to the psychiatrist, "that I can't sing; I can't dance; I can't tell jokes; I can't act; I can't play an instrument or juggle or do magic tricks or do anything!"

"Then why don't you give up show-business?"

"I can't – I'm a star!"

A tramp knocked on the back door of a house and asked for a bite to eat.

"Go away," said the lady of the house, "I never feed tramps."

"That's all right lady," said the tramp, "I'll feed myself."

Doctor, doctor! You've taken out my tonsils, my adenoids, my gall-bladder, my varicose veins and my appendix, but I still don't feel well.

That's quite enough out of you.

Little Jackie's mother was on the telephone to the boy's dentist.

"I don't understand it," she complained, "I thought his treatment would only cost me $10, but you've charged me $40."

"It is usually $10, madam," agreed the dentist, "but Jackie yelled so loudly that three of my other patients ran away!"

Three men were on trial, and the judge,
who had a terrible squint, said to the first,
"How do you plead?"
"Not guilty," said the second.
"I'm not talking to you," snapped the judge.
"I didn't say a word," said the third.

Fantasy
Figures

Did you hear about the monster who ate bits of metal every night?
It was his staple diet.

If a flying saucer is an aircraft, does that make a flying broomstick a witchcraft?

How do you get a ghost to lie perfectly flat?
You use a spirit level.

What do you call a ghost who only haunts the Town Hall?
The nightmayor.

Monster: Stick 'em down.
Ghost: Don't you mean, stick 'em up?
Monster: No wonder I'm not making much
money in this business.

What do you call a skeleton who goes out in
the snow and rain without a coat or an
umbrella?
A numbskull.

What did the werewolf eat after he'd had
his teeth taken out?
The dentist.

Mommy, mommy, what's a vampire?
Be quiet, dear, and drink your soup before it clots.

Why don't ghosts make good magicians?
You can see right through their tricks.

Did the bionic monster have a brother?
No, but he had lots of trans-sisters.

What did Frankenstein's monster say when he was struck by lightning?
"Thanks, I needed that."

What did E.T's mother say to him when he got home?
Where on Earth have you been?

What do you get if you cross a zombie with a boy scout?
A creature that scares old ladies across the road.

Ghost: Are you coming to my party?
Spook: Where is it?
Ghost: In the morgue – you know what they say, the morgue the merrier.

The ghost teacher was giving her pupils instructions on how to haunt a house properly. "Has everyone got the hang of walking through walls?" she asked. One little ghoul at the front of the class looked uncertain.

"Just watch the blackboard everyone," instructed the teacher, "and I'll go through it once more."

A monster decided to become a TV star, so he went to see an agent. "What do you do?" asked the agent.

"Bird impressions," said the monster.

"What kind of bird impressions?"

"I eat worms."

Igor: Only this morning Dr Frankenstein completed another amazing operation. He crossed an ostrich with a centipede.
Dracula: And what did he get?
Igor: We don't know – we haven't managed to catch it yet.

Did you hear about the monster who was known as Captain Kirk?
He had a left ear, a right ear and a final front ear.

Where does Dracula keep his savings?
In the blood bank.

Did you hear about the skeleton which was attacked by the dog?
It ran off with some bones and left him without a leg to stand on.

What did the werewolf write at the bottom of the letter?
Best vicious . . .

Woman in bed: Aaagh! Aaagh! A ghost just floated into my room!
Ghost: Don't worry, madam, I'm just passing through.

A monster walked into a shop selling dress fabrics and said, "I'd like six meters of pink satan for my wife."

"It's satin, sir, not satan," said the assistant. "Satan is something that looks like the devil."

"Oh," said the monster, "you know my wife?"

Teacher: What do you know about Lake Erie?
Rose: It's full of ghosts, Miss.

What happened when the werewolf met the five-headed monster?
It was love at first fright.

What airline do vampires travel on?
British Scareways.

What did the mother ghost say to the naughty baby ghost?
Spook when you're spooken to.

A horrible old witch surprised all her friends by announcing that she was going to get married. "But," said another old hag, "you always said men were stupid. And you vowed never to marry."
"Yes, I know," said the witch. "But I finally found one who asked me."

Why are vampires artistic?
They're good at drawing blood.

What did one skeleton say to the other?
If we had any guts we'd get out of here.

What happened when Dr Frankenstein
swallowed some uranium?
He got atomic ache.

Why did the wooden monsters stand in a
circle?
They were having a board meeting.

Dr Frankenstein decided to build an extension to his laboratory, so he crossed a cement mixer, a ghoul and a chicken. Now he's got a demon bricklayer.

What is even more invisible than the invisible ghost?
His shadow.

What's a skeleton?
Bones with the person off.

Why are Martians green?
Because they forgot to take their travel-sickness tablets.

What does Dracula say to his victims?
It's been nice gnawing you.

Why did Dracula eat strong peppermints?
Because he had bat breath.

Ghost: Do you believe in the hereafter?
Phantom: Of course I do.
Ghost: Well, hereafter leave me alone.

Did you hear about the little spook who
couldn't sleep at night because his brother
kept telling him human stories?

Robot: I have to dry my feet carefully
after a bath.
Monster: Why?
Robot: Otherwise I get rusty nails.

What kind of ghosts haunt hospitals?
Surgical spirits.

Two people went into a very dark, spooky cave. "I can't see a thing," said one.

"Hold my hand," said the other.

"All right." The first man reached out. "Take off that horrible bristly glove first, though."

"But I'm not wearing a glove . . ."

Did you hear about the competition to find the laziest spook in the world? All the competitors were lined up on stage. "I've got a really nice, easy job for the laziest person here," said the organizer. "Will the laziest spook raise his hand?"

All the spooks put up their hands – except one.

"Why didn't you raise your hand?" asked the presenter.

"Too much trouble," yawned the spook!

A short, fat, hairy monster was waiting for a train and decided to while away the time by weighing himself on a machine on the station platform. Once he'd weighed himself he looked at the chart that indicated the ideal weight for each height. "Having any problems?" asked another passenger. "Are you overweight?"
"No," said the monster, "I'm just four feet too short."

Which day of the week do ghosts like best?
Moandays.

How do phantom hens dance?
Chick to chick.

What's the best way of avoiding infection
from biting ghosts?
Don't bite any ghosts.

What do you get if you try to take a
ghost's photograph?
Transparencies.

Who speaks at the ghosts' press
conference?
The spooksperson.

What is a ghost's favorite dessert?
Boo-berry pie with I-scream.

Why are ghosts invisible?
They wear see-through clothes.

Why is the graveyard such a noisy place?
Because of all the coffin!

What do you get if you cross a ghost with
a packet of crisps?
Snacks that go crunch in the night.

Which weight do ghosts box at?
Phantom weight.

Why did the witch put her broom in the washing machine?
She wanted a clean sweep.

What do you call a wizard from outer space?
A flying sorcerer.

What do you call a motor bike belonging to a witch?
A brrooooom stick.

Why do skeletons drink milk?
Because it's good for the bones.

Why was Dracula so happy at the races?
His horse won by a neck.

What do you get if you cross a vampire
with Al Capone?
A fangster!

How does a vampire enter his house?
Through the bat flap.

How does a vampire get through life with
only one fang?
He has to grin and bare it.

How did skeletons send each other letters
in the days of the Wild West?
By Bony Express.

What happens to a witch when she loses
her temper?
She flies off the handle.

Why do skeletons hate winter?
Because the cold goes right through them.

Why are skeletons usually so calm?
Nothing gets under their skin.

Word Play

Flash Harry gave his girlfriend a mink stole for her birthday. Well, it may not have been mink, but it's fairly certain it was stole.

What should you give short elves?
Elf-raising flour.

Why is classroom like an old car?
Because it's full of nuts, and has a crank at the front.

Where can you dance in California?
San Fran-disco.

What did the children do when there were rock cakes for lunch?
Took their pick.

1st undertaker: I've just been given the sack.
2nd undertaker: Why?
1st undertaker: I buried someone in the wrong place.
2nd undertaker: That was a grave mistake.

Did you hear about the florist who had two children?
One's a budding genius and the other's a blooming idiot.

How do we know that Rome was built at night?
Because all the books say it wasn't built in a day!

Ben's dad was building a pine bookcase, and Ben was watching and occasionally helping.
"What are the holes for?" Ben asked.
"They're knot holes," said his dad.
"What are they, then, if they're not holes?" said Ben.

Which two letters are rotten for your teeth?
D K.

What's the difference between a square peg in a round hole and a kilo of lard?
One's a fat lot of good and the other's a good lot of fat!

What happens when business is slow at a medicine factory?
You can hear a cough drop.

What do you get if you cross a witch with an ice cube?
A cold spell.

Why do barbers make good drivers?
Because they know all the short cuts.

What did the "just married" spiders call their new home?
Newlywebs.

Sign on the school noticeboard: Guitar for sale, cheap, no strings attached.

Darren, at school dinner: I've just swallowed a bone.
Teacher: Are you choking?
Darren: No, I'm serious.

Girl: Shall I put the kettle on?
Boy: No, I think you look all right in the dress you're wearing.

What do you get if you cross a caretaker
with a monk who smokes large cigars?
A caretaker with a bad habit.

Who carries a sack and bites people?
Santa Jaws

Sign outside the school caretaker's hut:
Will the person who took my ladder please
return it, or further steps will be taken.

When George left school he was going to
be a printer. All the teachers said he was
the right type.

What's the difference between an iced lolly and the school bully?
You lick one, the others lick you.

Man to waiter: A pork chop, please, and make it lean.
Waiter: Certainly, Mr Smith, which way?

Why did the man go out and buy a set of tools?
Because everyone kept telling him he had a screw loose.

What's the difference between a nail and a boxer?
One gets knocked in, the other gets knocked out.

A pilot flying over the jungle was having trouble with his plane and decided to bail out before it crashed. So he got into his parachute, jumped, pulled the rip-cord, and drifted gently down to land. Unfortunately he landed right in a large cooking pot which a tribal chief was simmering gently over a fire. The chief looked at him, rubbed his eyes, looked again, and asked, "What's this flier doing in my soup?"

Two fleas were sitting on Robinson Crusoe's back as he lay on the beach in the sun. "Well, so long," said one to the other, "I'll see you on Friday."

Two fishermen were out in their boat one day when a hand appeared in the ocean. "What's that?" asked the first fisherman. "It looks as if someone's drowning!" "Nonsense," said the second. "It was just a little wave."

What kind of bandage do people wear after heart surgery?
Ticker tape.

Did you hear about Mrs Dimwit's new baby? She thought babies should be pink, so she took this one to the doctor because it was a horrible yeller.

What happened to Ray when a ten-ton truck ran over him?
He became X-Ray.

Did you hear about the boy who got worried when his nose grew to eleven inches long?
He thought it might turn into a foot.

What do you do if you split your sides laughing?
Run until you get a stitch.

Do undertakers enjoy their job?
Of corpse they do.

Teacher: Didn't you know the bell had gone?
Silly Sue: I didn't take it, Miss.

Hil: Who was the fastest runner in history?
Bill: Adam. He was first in the human race.

Did you hear about the teacher who was trying to instil good table manners in her girls? She told them, "A well-brought-up girl never crumbles her bread or rolls in her soup."

Did you hear about the boy who was told to do 100 lines? He drew 100 cats on the paper. He thought the teacher had said "lions."

What's your handicrafts teacher like? She's a sew and sew.

What gets bigger the more you take away? A hole.

Why did the undertaker chop all his
corpses into little bits?
Because he liked them to rest in pieces.

Why was the insect thrown out of the
forest?
Because he was a litter bug.

What did the undertaker say to his
girlfriend?
Em-balmy about you.

What happened when the pussy swallowed
a penny?
There was money in the kitty.

A young lad was helping his dad with do-it-yourself jobs around the house. "You know, son," said the father, "you're just like lightning with that hammer."

"Fast, eh?" said the boy.

"Oh, no – you never strike in the same place twice."

What did the traffic light say to the motorist?

Don't look now, I'm changing.

What's the difference between a Peeping Tom and someone who's just got out of the bath?

One is rude and nosey. The other is nude and rosey.

Why did the lazy idiot apply for a job in a bakery?
He fancied a long loaf.

What's the difference between a sigh, a car and a monkey?
A sigh is oh dear. A car is too dear. A monkey is you, dear.

Was the carpenter's son a chip off the old block?

Do you serve women in this bar?
No sir, you have to bring your own.

What happens if you play table-tennis with
a bad egg?
First it goes ping, then it goes pong.

Who is Wyatt Burp?
The sheriff with the repeater.

Why are school cooks cruel?
Because they batter fish and beat eggs.

What's a giant's favorite tale?
A tall story.

My sister thinks that a juggernaut is an empty beer mug.

What's the difference between a crossword expert, a greedy boy and a pot of glue?
A crossword expert is a good puzzler and the greedy boy's a pud guzzler. The pot of glue? Ah, that's where you get stuck.

What did the Eskimo children sing when their principal was leaving?
"Freeze a Jolly Good Fellow."

Ben's teacher regards Ben as a wonder child. He wonders whether he'll ever learn anything.

What's the difference between a kangaroo, a lumberjack and a bag of peanuts?
A kangaroo hops and chews and a lumberjack chops and hews.
Yes, but what's the bag of peanuts for?
For monkeys like you.

What do you get if you cross a burglar
with a concrete mixer?
A hardened criminal.

Who makes suits and eats spinach?
Popeye the Tailorman.

Where does Tarzan buy his clothes?
At a Jungle Sale.

Is this a second-hand shop?
Yes, sir.
Good. Can you fit one on my watch, please?

What is a mermaid?
A deep-she fish.

What kind of cans are there in Mexico?
Mexicans.

In the park this morning I was surrounded
by lions.
Lions! In the park?
Yes – dandelions!

Notice (in a new shop window): Don't go
elsewhere and be robbed – try us!

Jennifer: Are you coming to my party?
Sandra: No, I ain't going.
Jennifer: Now, you know what Miss told us.
Not ain't. It's I am not going, he is not
going, she is not going, they are not going.
Sandra: Blimey, ain't nobody going?

Passer-by (to fisherman): Is this river any
good for fish?
Fisherman: It must be. I can't get any of
them to leave it.

They're not going to grow bananas any
longer.
Really? Why not?
Because they're long enough already.

I wonder where I got that puncture?
Maybe it was at that last fork in the
road . . .

"Gosh, it's raining cats and dogs," said
Suzie looking out of the kitchen window.
"I know," said her mother who had just
come in. "I've just stepped in a poodle!"

A noise woke me up this morning.
What was that?
The crack of dawn.

Why is perfume obedient?
Because it is scent wherever it goes.

Which soldiers smell of salt and pepper?
Seasoned troopers.

A man with a newt on his shoulder walked into a pub. "What do you call him?" asked the barmaid. "Tiny," said the man.
"Why do you call him Tiny?"
"Because he's my newt!"

What do you get if you cross a nun and a chicken?
A pecking order.

What does Luke Skywalker shave with?
A laser blade.

Which capital city cheats at exams?
Peking.

Why did the woman take a load of hay to bed?
To feed her nightmare.

What happened when the wheel was invented?
It caused a revolution.

Ivan: What are you reading?
Andrea: It's a book about electricity.
Ivan: Oh, current events?
Andrea: No, light reading.

How did Benjamin Franklin discover electricity?
It came to him in a flash.

Where do geologists go for entertainment?
To rock concerts.

Why is history the sweetest lesson?
Because it's full of dates.

What's wrong with this fish?
Long time, no sea.

What did the tie say to the hat?
You go on ahead and I'll hang around.

What did the picture say to the wall?
I've got you covered.

Why did the man take a pencil to bed?
To draw the curtains . . . I'd tell you
another joke about a pencil, but it hasn't
any point.

Why did the burglar take a shower?
He wanted to make a clean getaway.

Why do idiots eat biscuits?
Because they're crackers.

"What is your occupation?" asked the
magistrate.
"I'm a locksmith, your honor."
"And what were you doing in the jeweler's
shop at three in the morning when the
police officers entered?"
"Making a bolt for the door!"

What do you call an American drawing?
Yankee Doodle.

A Dubliner was in court charged with parking his car in a restricted area. The judge asked if he had anything to say in his defense. "They shouldn't put up such misleading notices," said the Dubliner. "It said FINE FOR PARKING HERE."

What do you call an American with a lavatory on his head?
John.

What's the name for a short-legged tramp?
A low-down bum.

Why is it not safe to sleep on trains?
Because they run over sleepers.

Sign in a café: All drinking water in this establishment has been personally passed by the management.

Did you hear about the farmer's boy who hated the country?
He went to the big city and got a job as a shoe-shine boy, so the farmer made hay while the son shone!

What did the Ancient Greeks shout when
Archimedes fell in a dung-heap?
You Reeka! You Reeka!

Did you her about the man who fell into an
upholstery machine?
He's fully recovered.

Numbskulls

A stupid glazier was examining a broken window. He looked at it for a while and then said: "It's worse than I thought. It's broken on both sides."

"How do you keep a stupid person happy for hours?"
"Give him a piece of paper with 'please turn over' written on both sides."

Did you hear about the man who hijacked a submarine?
He demanded a million dollars and a parachute.

When he received the end-of-term report Brenda's father went crazy. "This report is terrible," he said, "I'm not at all pleased with it."

"I told the teacher you wouldn't like it," said Brenda, "but he insisted on sending it just the same."

Why is the stupid red-headed boy like a biscuit?
Because he's a ginger nut.

Why do stupid people eat biscuits?
Because they're crackers.

Why did the robot act stupid?
Because he had a screw loose.

My mother is so stupid that she thinks a string quartet is four people playing tennis.

A man telephoned London Airport. "How long does it take to get to New York?"
"Just a minute."
"Thanks very much."

My friend is so stupid that he thinks twice before saying nothing.

Why did the stupid sailor grab a bar of soap when his ship sank?
He thought he could wash himself ashore.

Did you hear about the sailor that was discharged from the submarine service?
He was caught sleeping with the windows open.

An idiotic laborer was told by an equally idiotic foreman to dig a hole in the road.
"And what shall I do with the earth, sir?" asked the laborer.
"Don't be daft, man," he replied. "Just dig another hole and bury it."

Did you hear about the stupid motorist
who always drove his car in reverse?
It was because he knew the Highway Code
backward.

A stupid bank robber rushed into a bank,
pointed two fingers at the clerk and said:
"This is a muck up."
"Don't you mean a stick up?" asked the girl.
"No," said the robber, "it's a muck up. I've
forgotten my gun."

How do you confuse an idiot?
Give him two spades and ask him to take
his pick.

A stupid man spent the evening with some friends, but when the time came for him to leave, a terrific storm started with thunder, lightning and torrential rain. "You can't go home in this," said the host, "you'd better stay the night."

"That's very kind of you," said the man, "I'll just pop home and get my pajamas."

Doctor: And did you drink your medicine after your bath, Mrs Soap?

Mrs Soap: No, doctor. By the time I'd drunk the bath there wasn't room for medicine.

A mountaineer fell down a very deep crevasse, breaking both his arms. Another member of the party managed to lower a rope until it was just within reach of the man's head.

"Quick!" he shouted. "Get hold of the rope with your teeth and I'll pull you up." Inch by painful inch, the mountaineer was dragged back up the crevasse. When he only had two feet to go, his rescuer called out, "Are you all right?"

"Yes, aaaaaaaaarrrrrrrrgggggghhh hhhh!" came the reply.

Waiter, waiter, this lobster's only got one claw.
It must have been in a fight, sir.
Then bring me the winner.

My sister is so stupid she thinks that aroma is someone who travels a lot.

Did you hear about the idiot who won the Tour de France?
He did a lap of honor.

An idiot decided to start a chicken farm so he bought a hundred chickens to start. A month later he returned to the dealer for another hundred chickens because all of the first lot had died. A month later he was back at the dealer's for another hundred chickens for the second lot had also died. "But I think I know where I'm going wrong," said the idiot. "I think I'm planting them too deep."

Did you hear about the idiotic karate champion who joined the army?
The first time he saluted, he nearly killed himself.

Sandra's mother said no young man in his right mind would take her to the school dance in her bikini, so she decided to go with her friend's stupid brother.

My big brother is such an idiot. The other day I saw him hitting himself on the head with a hammer. He was trying to make his head swell so his hat wouldn't fall over his eyes.

My sister is so dumb, she thinks that a buttress is a female goat.

How does an idiot call for his dog?
He puts two fingers in his mouth and then shouts Rover.

My friend is so stupid he thinks that an autograph is a chart showing sales figures for cars.

Why did the idiots' tug o' war team lose the match?
They pushed.

Teacher: You weren't at school last Friday, Robert. I heard you were out playing football.

Robert: That's not true, Sir. And I've got the cinema tickets to prove it.

Wally Woollynut was given the job of painting a flagpole but he didn't know how much paint he would need. "Lay it down and measure it," suggested a mate.

"That's no good," said Wally, "I need to know the height, not the length."

Did you hear about the idiot who had a new bath put in? The plumber said, "Would you like a plug for it?"
The idiot replied, "Oh, I didn't know it was electric."

Did you hear what Dumb Donald did when he offered to paint the garage for his dad in the summer holidays?
The instructions said "put on three coats," so he went in and put on his blazer, his raincoat and his duffel coat.

Did you hear about the utterly brainless monster who sat on the floor?
He fell off.

Did you hear about the stupid photographer?
He saved burned-out lightbulbs for use in his darkroom.

The math teacher and the English teacher went out for a quick pizza after school.
"How long will the pizzas be?" asked the math teacher.
"Sorry, Sir," replied the waiter, "we don't do long pizzas, just ordinary round ones."

Wilberforce Witherspoon saw a notice outside a police station which read: MAN WANTED FOR ROBBERY. So he went in and applied for the job!

My dad is stupid. He thinks a fjord is a
Norwegian motor car.

Jimmy, how many more times must I tell
you to come away from that biscuit barrel?
No more, mom. It's empty.

What's red, runs on wheels and eats grass?
A bus. I lied about the grass.

Did you hear about the village idiot buying
bird seed?
He said he wanted to grow some birds.

I can't understand the critics saying that only an idiot would like that television program. I really enjoyed it.

Father: Would you like a pocket calculator for Christmas, son?
Danny: No thanks, Dad. I know how many pockets I've got.

At the scene of a bank raid the police sergeant came running up to his inspector and said, "He got away, sir!"
The inspector was furious. "But I told you to put a man on all the exits!" he roared. "How could he have got away?"
"He left by one of the entrances, sir!"

Did you hear about the stupid tap dancer?
He fell in the sink.

A stupid man was struggling out of his house with a big table. His neighbor said to him, "Hello, Harry. Where are you going with that then?"
And Harry replied, "I'm taking it to the draper's shop to have it measured for a new tablecloth."

On their first evening in their new home the bride went in to the kitchen to fix the drinks. Five minutes later she came back into the living-room in tears.

"What's the matter, my angel?" asked her husband anxiously.

"Oh Derek!" she sobbed, "I put the ice cubes in hot water to wash them and now they've disappeared!"

A doctor had been attending a rich old man for some time, but it became apparent that the old chap had not long to live. Accordingly, the doctor advised his wealthy patient to put his affairs in order.

"Oh yes, I've done that," said the old gentleman. "I've only got to make my will. And do you know what I'm going to do with all my money? I'm going to leave it to the doctor who saves my life . . ."

Vincent, why have you got a sausage stuck behind your ear?
Eh? Oh no, I must have eaten my pencil for lunch!

A man rushed into the doctor's office, jumped on the doctor's back, and started screaming "One! Two! Three! Four!"
"Wait a minute!" yelled the doctor, struggling to free himself. "What do you think you're doing?"
"Well, doctor," said the eccentric man, "they did say I could count on you!"

Simple Simon was writing a geography essay. It began, "The people who live in Paris are called parasites . . ."

The criminal mastermind found one of his gang sawing the legs off his bed. "What are you doing that for?" demanded the crook boss.

"Only doing what you ordered," said the stupid thug. "You told me to lie low for a bit!"

A jeweler standing behind the counter of his shop was astounded to see a man come hurtling head-first through the window. "What on earth are you up to?" he demanded.

"I'm terribly sorry," said the man, "I forgot to let go of the brick!"

John kept pestering his parents to buy a video, but they said they couldn't afford one. So one day John came home clutching a package containing a brand-new video. "Wherever did you get the money to pay for that?" asked his father suspiciously. "It's all right, Dad," replied John, "I traded the TV in for it."

Classroom
Jokes

Alec turned up for football practice clutching a large broom.

"What's that for?" asked the coach.

"You said I was going to be sweeper today."

"Ann! Point out Australia for me on the map."

Ann went to the front of the class, picked up the pointer and showed the rest of the class where Australia was.

"Well done! Now, Alec! Can you tell us who discovered Australia?"

"Er . . . Ann, Miss?"

"Teacher is a bore!" was scrawled on the blackboard one day.

"I do not want to see that on my blackboard," he thundered when he saw it.

"Sorry, Sir! I didn't realize you wanted it kept secret."

"And what might your name be?" the school secretary asked the new boy.

"Well it might be Cornelius, but it's not. It's Sam."

What happens if there's a collision outside school?

There's usually a fight.

What happened to the baby chicken that misbehaved at school?
It was eggspelled.

Teacher: I was going to read you a story called "The Invasion of the Body Snatchers," but I've changed my mind.
Class: Oh why, Miss?
Teacher: Because we might get carried away.

"Ann," said the dancing mistress. "There are two things stopping you becoming the world's greatest ballerina?"
"What are they, Miss?" asked Ann.
"Your feet."

"I hope you're not one of those boys who sits and watches the school clock," said the principal to a new boy.
"No, Sir. I've got a digital watch that bleeps at half past three."

What's the definition of a school report?
A poison pen letter from the principal.

Why did the soccer teacher give his team lighters?
Because they kept losing all their matches.

What's the difference between school lunches and a bucket of fresh manure?
School lunches are usually cold.

What's the longest piece of furniture in the school?
The multiplication table.

Did you hear about the cross-eyed teacher
who had no control over her pupils?

Miss Jones who teaches us maths,
Isn't a bundle of laughs.
For, sad to tell,
She doesn't half smell,
For she never seems to take any baths.

What do you get if you cross old potatoes
with lumpy stew?
School lunches.

Did you hear about the teacher who married the dairy maid?
It didn't last. They were like chalk and cheese.

"Why are you crying Amanda?" asked her teacher.
"'Cos Jenny's broken my new doll, Miss," she cried.
"How did she do that?"
"I hit her on the head with it."

Did you hear about the teacher who retired?
His class gave him an illuminated address.
They burned his house down.

Confucius he say: If teacher ask you question and you not know answer, mumble.

What did the arithmetic book say to the geometry book?
Boy! Do we have our problems!

"And what's your name?" the secretary asked the next new boy.
"Butter."
"I hope your first name's not Roland," smirked the secretary.
"No, Miss. It's Brendan."

"What's your first name?" the teacher asked a new boy.

It's Orson, Miss. I was named after Orson Welles, the film star."

"Just as well your last name's not Cart. Isn't it?"

"Yes Miss. It's Trapp."

Did you hear about the math teacher who fainted in class?

Everyone tried to bring her 2.

A little girl was next in line. "My name's Curtain," she said.

"I hope your first name's not Annette?"

"No. It's Velvet."

What's the difference between a boring teacher and a boring book?
You can shut the book up.

Teacher: That's the stupidest boy in the whole school.
Mother: That's my son.
Teacher: Oh! I'm so sorry.
Mother: You're sorry?

"Oh I'm sorry. I didn't realize you were her mother.
"I'm not. I'm her father actually! And she's my son!"

Typing teacher: Bob! Your work has certainly improved. There are only ten mistakes here.

Bob: Oh good, Miss.

Teacher: Now let's look at the second line, shall we?

A teacher in a country school received the following letter from the mother of one of his students:

Dear Teacher,

Please excuse Phil from school last week. His father was ill and the pig had to be fed.

Yours sincerely,

Why are art galleries like retirement homes for teachers?
Because they're both full of old masters.

It was sweltering hot outside. The teacher came into the classroom wiping his brow and said, "Ninety-two today. Ninety-two." "Happy birthday to you. Happy birthday to you. . ." sang the class.

Did you hear about the brilliant geography teacher?
He had abroad knowledge of his subject.

"What's your father's occupation?" asked the school secretary on the first day of the new term.

"He's a conjurer, Miss," said the new boy.

"How interesting. What's his favorite trick?"

"He saws people in half."

"Golly! Now next question. Any brothers and sisters?"

"One half-brother and two half-sisters."

Billy's mother was called into the school one day by the principal.

"We're very worried about Billy," he said. "He goes round all day 'cluck, cluck, clucking'."

"That's right," said Billy's mother. "He thinks he's a chicken."

"Haven't you taken him to a psychiatrist?"

"Well we would, but we need the eggs."

Two elderly teachers were talking over old times and saying how much things had changed. "I mean," said the first, "I caught one of the boys kissing one of the girls yesterday."

"Extraordinary," said the second. "I didn't even kiss my wife before I married her, did you?"

"I can't remember. What was her maiden name?"

"Please Sir. There's something wrong with my stomach."

"Well button up your jacket and no one will notice."

"Now remember boys and girls," said the science teacher. "You can tell a tree's age by counting the rings in a cross section. One ring for each year."

Alec went home for tea and found a Swiss Roll on the table.

"I'm not eating that, Mom," he said. "It's five years old."

A warning to any young sinner,
Be you fat or perhaps even thinner.
If you do not repent,
To Hell you'll be sent.
With nothing to eat but school dinner.

A mother was desperate to get her under-age daughter into kindergarten and was trying to impress the headmistress with the child's intellectual abilities. "She'll easily keep up with the others even though she is a year younger."

"Well," said the teacher doubtfully. "Could she prove it by saying something?"

"Certainly Miss," said the child. "Something pertaining to your conversation, or something purely irrelevant?"

How do Religious Education teachers mark exams?
With spirit levels.

Teacher's strong; teacher's gentle.
Teacher's kind. And I am mental.

Why did the science teacher marry the
school cleaner?
Because she swept him off his feet.

Please Sir! Please Sir! Why do you keep me locked up in this cage?
Because you're the teacher's pet.

Teacher: Are you good at arithmetic?
Mary: Well, yes and no.
Teacher: What do you mean, yes and no?
Mary: Yes, I'm no good at arithmetic.

Why is a pencil the heaviest thing in your bag?
Because it's full of lead.

Mrs Jones: Well, Billy, how are you getting along with the trampolining?
Billy: Oh, up and down, you know.

Mandy: Our teacher went on a special banana diet.
Andy: Did she lose weight?
Mandy: No, but she couldn't half climb trees well!

Art teacher: What color would you paint the sun and the wind?
Brian: The sun rose, and the wind blue.

Teacher: Your books are a disgrace, Archibald. I don't see how anyone can possibly make as many mistakes in one day as you do.

Archibald: I get here early, Sir.

When is an English teacher like a judge? When she hands out long sentences.

Geography teacher: What mineral do we import from America?

Daft Darren: Coca-Cola!

What's black and white and horrible?
A math examination paper.

What nickname did the police give to the
new blonde woman police officer?
A fair cop.

Kelly: Is God a doctor, Miss?
Teacher: In some ways, Kelly. Why do you
ask?
Kelly: Because the Bible says that the Lord
gave the tablets to Moses.

How can you tell when it's rabbit pie for
school dinner?
It has hares in it.

George knocked on the door of his friend's house. When his friend's mother answered he said: "Can Albert come out to play?"
"No," said the mother, "it's too cold."
"Well, then," said George "can his football come out to play?"

What is brown, hairy, wears dark glasses and carries a pile of exercise books?
A coconut disguised as a teacher.

Why did the teacher put corn in his shoes?
Because he had pigeon toes.

What do you call a deaf teacher?
Anything you like, he can't hear you.

How can a teacher double his money?
By folding it in half.

Teacher: What is an Indian's home called?
Andy: I don't know, Miss, but I know what a little Indian's joke is called.
Teacher: Well, what is it called?
Andy: A Minihaha.

Girl: My teacher's a peach.
Mother: You mean she's sweet.
Girl: No, she has a heart of stone.

Headmaster: I've called you into my office, Peter, because I want to talk to you about two words I wish you wouldn't use so often. One is "great" and the other is "lousy."
Peter: Certainly Sir. What are they?

Mother: How was your first day at school?
Little Boy: OK, but I haven't got my present yet.
Mother: What do you mean?
Little Boy: Well the teacher gave me a chair, and said "Sit there for the present."

Teacher to pupil: How many thousand times have I told you not to exaggerate?

Did you hear about the schoolboy who just couldn't get to grips with decimals?
He couldn't see the point.

Father: Jennifer, I've had a letter from your principal. It seems you've been neglecting your appearance.
Jennifer: Dad?
Father: He says you haven't appeared in school all week.

Teacher: What happened to your homework?
Boy: I made it into a paper plane and someone hijacked it.

Tom: Why are you scratching your head?
Harry: I've got those arithmetic bugs again.
Tom: Arithmetic bugs – what are they?
Harry: Well, some people call them head lice.
Tom: Then why do you call them arithmetic bugs?
Harry: Because they add to my misery, subtract from my pleasure, divide my attention and multiply like crazy.

Teacher: What's the best way to pass this geometry test?
Boy: Knowing all the angles?

Teacher: You should have been here at nine o'clock.

Boy: Why? Did something happen?

Mother: What did you learn at school today?

Son: Not enough. I have to go back tomorrow.

Teacher: If I had ten flies on my desk, and I swatted one, how many flies would be left?

Girl: One – the dead one!

One unfortunate teacher started off a lesson with the following instruction, "I want you all to give me a list of the lower animals, starting with Georgina Clark . . ."

Music master: Brian, if "f" means forte, what does "ff" mean?
Brian: Eighty!

"Frank," said the weary math teacher, "if you had seven dollars in your pocket, and seven dollars in another pocket, what would you have?"
"Someone else's trousers on!"

Teacher: Martin, I've taught you everything I know, and you're still ignorant!

Teacher: Ford, you're late for school again. What is it this time?
Ford: I sprained my ankle, sir.
Teacher: That's a lame excuse.